Courageous Generosity

Courageous Generosity

A Bible Study for Women on Heroic Sacrifice

by Stacy Mitch

EMMAUS
ROAD
PUBLISHING

Steubenville, Ohio
www.emmausroad.org

Emmaus Road Publishing
1468 Parkview Circle
Steubenville, Ohio 43952

Library of Congress Control Number: 2009937739
ISBN: 978-1-931018-57-9

Cover design and layout by
Theresa Westling

Cover artwork:
Réunion des Musées Nationaux / Art Resource, NY

To my Dad and Mom:
Wayne and Marcella Cairns

CONTENTS

ABBREVIATIONS

Old Testament
Gen./Genesis
Ex./Exodus
Lev./Leviticus
Num./Numbers
Deut./Deuteronomy
Josh./Joshua
Judg./Judges
Ruth/Ruth
1 Sam./1 Samuel
2 Sam./2 Samuel
1 Kings/1 Kings
2 Kings/2 Kings
1 Chron./1 Chronicles
2 Chron./2 Chronicles
Ezra/Ezra
Neh./Nehemiah
Tob./Tobit
Jud./Judith
Esther/Esther
Job/Job
Ps./Psalms
Prov./Proverbs
Eccles./Ecclesiastes
Song/Song of Solomon
Wis./Wisdom
Sir./Sirach (Ecclesiasticus)
Is./Isaiah
Jer./Jeremiah
Lam./Lamentations
Bar./Baruch

Ezek./Ezekiel
Dan./Daniel
Hos./Hosea
Joel/Joel
Amos/Amos
Obad./Obadiah
Jon./Jonah
Mic./Micah
Nahum/Nahum
Hab./Habakkuk
Zeph./Zephaniah
Hag./Haggai
Zech./Zechariah
Mal./Malachi
1 Mac./1 Maccabees
2 Mac./2 Maccabees

New Testament
Mt./Matthew
Mk./Mark
Lk./Luke
Jn./John
Acts/Acts of the Apostles
Rom./Romans
1 Cor./1 Corinthians
2 Cor./2 Corinthians
Gal./Galatians
Eph./Ephesians
Phil./Philippians
Col./Colossians

1 Thess./1 Thessalonians
2 Thess./2 Thessalonians
1 Tim./1 Timothy
2 Tim./2 Timothy
Tit./Titus
Philem./Philemon
Heb./Hebrews
Jas./James
1 Pet./1 Peter
2 Pet./2 Peter
1 Jn./1 John
2 Jn./2 John
3 Jn./3 John
Jude/Jude
Rev./Revelation (Apocalypse)

PREFACE

Catholics have traditions for just about everything—including how we decorate our homes. It's not that the Church tells us what color to paint the walls (although I admit, there are times I could probably use the help). Rather, what She offers us is some advice about what to hang on those walls—namely, crucifixes.

For centuries, Catholics have been encouraged to hang crucifixes throughout their homes. And as the years have gone by, more and more crucifixes have found their way into my own home. And whenever I feel like more is being asked of me than I can give, whenever the task at hand seems too great, my eyes now automatically seek out the crucifix in the room. There, I see Jesus, the all-powerful God of the universe, hanging from a piece of wood, pierced and bloodied, mocked and scorned. I see Jesus who gave everything He had and was to the Father. I see Jesus who gave everything for me. And I remember that, if I want to be with Jesus one day, I have to give everything too.

Needless to say, I have come to understand the wisdom of hanging crucifixes throughout the house. Each and every one is a reminder that the path to holiness for all Christians is heroic generosity. In imitation of Our Lord and Savior, we are called to give our hearts, our minds, and our lives to God. We are also called to pour ourselves out in love for those around us—our families, our friends, and our neighbors. Fortunately for us, we have more than Jesus' example to help us in this task. We also have His grace, which guides us and sustains us along the way. This study is written to help you better understand what the call to heroic generosity means and reflect on what it might look like in your everyday life. It's also written to help you understand how, with God's grace, we can answer that call more faithfully, more willingly, and, above all, more joyfully.

Courageous Generosity

Blessed Mother Teresa of Calcutta lived for others. She begged for the poor. She fed the poor. She clothed the poor. She lavished her love on the sick, the deformed, and the dying—holding in her arms the men, women, and children who no one else would touch. She defended the right to life of the littlest and weakest among us, and she did it all while owning nothing herself, giving every gift she received to those most desperately in need. Courageous generosity defined the life of Blessed Teresa, just as it defined the life of John Paul II and all the Church's holy men and women. That's because sainthood demands courageous generosity. No one can be holy without it. But so much in our world and in our own hearts works against us learning to live that virtue.

Today, we live in a culture that glorifies selfishness. The television shows and movies we watch, the music we listen to, and the advertisements we see, all communicate the same message: It's all about me. We're encouraged to think of ourselves, not others, first, to do what we want regardless of what it costs others, to seek our own happiness before the happiness of others.

The great irony, of course, is that most of us don't need any encouragement from the culture to indulge our own selfish desires: Fallen human selfishness comes pretty easily. I know. I think I just might be an expert at it!

As Christian women, however, we need to reject the selfish inclinations of our hearts and the encouragement to selfishness coming at us from the culture and, instead, follow the example of Christ. At the Last Supper, Jesus washed the feet of the apostles, a job that only the lowliest of servants would do.[1] In doing

---

[1] See John 13:1–20.

that, He showed His followers that they, the future leaders of the Church, must stoop to serve all men and women, just as He, the God of the universe, stooped to serve them. He called them to practice courageous generosity. He still calls each of us to that same task.

Does that mean we are all to live as Mother Teresa did? No. *And yes.* Obviously, God doesn't call each and every one of us to live with the poorest of the poor in the slums of Calcutta. He gives each of us our own gifts and talents and asks us to use them in many, many different ways in the service of Christ and His Church.[2] But, in whatever way He calls us to serve the Church, He still calls us to follow the example of Christ and the saints and live lives of courageous generosity. This is the narrow way taught by Jesus—the way that asks us to put ourselves second and Jesus first, the way that turns our hearts of stone to hearts of flesh and allows us see the face of our Beloved.[3] This is the way to holiness.

But what does that way look like? What does following it mean in practice, not just theory? That is the subject of our study.

Courage

Before we can live courageous generosity, we need to know what both courage and generosity are. Let's start with courage.

Throughout his pontificate, Pope John Paul II reminded us of Christ's words in Matthew 28, "Be not afraid!" Courage is the virtue that empowers us to "be not afraid"—to overcome our fear and do what we know we ought to do. That means the prerequisite of courage is fear! Fear always precedes the exercise of courage. When we act courageously, we do what we ought *in the face of and in spite of our fears*.

---

[2] See Romans 12:4–8.
[3] See Ezekiel 36:26.

Courageous Generosity 3

1. Read Joshua 1:1–9.

a. What did God ask Joshua to do?

_____

_____

b. The Lord repeatedly told Joshua, "Be strong and of good courage." Look back to Numbers 13:25–33. Why was this encouragement necessary? What obstacles would Joshua face?

_____

_____

c. The Lord knows that Joshua's task is intimidating and frightening. It's natural, in those circumstances, to feel fear. That's why He makes a promise to Joshua in Joshua 1:5. What does the Lord promise him? Isn't this a promise the Lord makes to us too?

_____

_____

d. God may never have asked you to take on the Canaanites in battle, but have you ever had a "Promised Land" challenge? How did you see the Lord work in your life as you trusted Him?

_____

_____

> "Consider seriously how quickly people change, and how little trust is to be had in them; and hold fast to God, who does not change."
>
> St. Theresa of Avila

2. Read Exodus 14:10–14.

a. As Pharaoh's army advanced, the Israelites were terrified.

What did they prefer in their fear?

_____

_____

b. Though not literal slaves like the Israelites in Egypt, we can easily become slaves to our fear. How is fear a form of slavery?

_____

_____

c. How have you experienced this in your own life? What fears have enslaved you?

_____

_____

3. Fear without courage can also prevent us from doing what we should. Read Matthew 26:47, 56 and 26:69–75.

a. What did the apostles do to our Lord in their fear?

_____

_____

b. In our secular post-Christian culture have you ever done the same? Explain.

_____

_____

c. What came out of that decision? Did it solve your problem or did it only create more difficulties?

_____

_____

"The principal act of courage is to endure and withstand dangers doggedly rather than to attack them."
St. Thomas Aquinas

4. According to the following passages what is the source of bondage? What is the source of freedom?

Galatians 4:4–8
Ephesians 1:3–8; 2:1–6
Colossians 1:13–14
James 3:13–18

_____

_____

5. Jesus repeatedly tells His followers, "Do not be afraid," "fear not," and "take courage." Read Matthew 10:29–31. On what basis should we take courage?

_____

_____

6. Read Romans 8:14–17. What does the author of Romans tell us we have received that should prevent us from becoming slaves to fear? What assistance does God give us in practicing courage?

_____

_____

7. How has courage set you free? What does freedom from fear empowers you to do or be?

_____

_____

Generosity

Just as we can only practice courage in the face of fear, we can only practice generosity in the face of need. But that need doesn't have to be material. It can also be spiritual, emotional, or relational. It's so easy to fall into the trap of thinking of generosity only in terms of dollars—how much we give to our parish or to the poor or even to our own children. That's part of generosity, a part we'll talk about later on in this study, but it's not what defines generosity. So what does define generosity?

8. Read the following passages.

Colossians 3:1
Romans 12:10–21; 15:1–3
Ephesians 4:1–3; 5:21
1 Thessalonians 5:13b–15
1 Timothy 6:18

a. What are we encouraged to do in each passage?

_____

_____

b. How do these actions exemplify generosity?

_____

_____

> "What does love look like? It has the hands to help others. It has the feet to hasten to the poor and needy. It has eyes to see misery and want. It has the ears to hear the sighs and sorrows of men. That is what love looks like."
>
> St. Augustine of Hippo

9. According to the following passages, what happens to those who are generous?

a. Proverbs 11:24–25: _____

b. Proverbs 22:9: _____

10. Think about the life of Christ. List at least three ways in which He set the example of heroic generosity.

_____

_____

11. Why is it difficult for us to be generous? What fears stop us from living the virtue of courageous generosity?

_____

_____

Memory Verse
"I will not fail you or forsake you. . . .
Only be strong and very courageous."
Joshua 1:5b, 7a

Sacrifice:
The Way to Joy

Childbirth is notoriously painful. The Bible refers to it repeatedly to emphasize struggle or agony. I also think it is the perfect example of the fruit of sacrifice. The suffering of labor gives way to tears of joy when a beautiful baby is cuddled in your arms. Pain is quickly forgotten and replaced with incalculable joy.

The athlete's pain is also well-known. "No pain, no gain," goes the saying familiar to all athletes. The temporary physical struggle is rewarded.

The same goes for spiritual struggles. In the end, the blessings of sacrifice outweigh the cost of the sacrifice In fact, the sacrifice leads us to joy. Truly, God has much to teach us about the beauty and blessings of sacrifice. Let's begin.

1. God is a Family of Three Persons, giving Themselves to each other in love through all eternity. Since we're made in God's image, we're called to give of ourselves as well. That's why before Adam and Eve fell from grace, giving came naturally; it was easy for humans. After the Fall, however, giving became a sacrifice. It became hard. God showed us this in the very first sacrifice ever made, a sacrifice made by Him.

Read Genesis 3:21.

a. What does God sacrifice in this passage?

_____

b. What did that sacrifice literally accomplish? What did it figuratively accomplish?

_____

_____

_____

c. What does this tell us about the relationship between sacrifice and sin?

_____

_____

_____

d. Have you ever made a sacrifice as a way of making atonement for something you've done wrong? Explain.

_____

_____

_____

Throughout the Old Testament, God's people continue to sacrifice animals as a way of atoning for their sins. God actually gave them explicit instructions about how to sacrifice and what to sacrifice in the Books of Exodus, Leviticus, and Deuteronomy. But atonement is not the only reason people made sacrifices in the Old Testament.

2. Read Genesis 6:17–18.

a. What did God promise Noah?

_____

b. Now read Genesis 7:2. What did God command Noah to bring with him?

_____

c. What did Noah do in Genesis 8:13–22? What was God's response? What does this tell us about the command God gave Noah in 7:2?

_____

_____

_____

_____

d. Why do you think God would require a sacrifice in these circumstances?

_____

_____

e. Have you ever offered a sacrifice of thanksgiving to God for a blessing that He has given you or your family?

Explain.

_____

_____

_____

_____

3. Read the story of God's dealings with Abraham in Genesis 17:16–19 and Hannah in 1 Samuel 1:9–19. Then read what God asks of Abraham in Genesis 22:1–19, and what Hannah does in 1 Samuel 1:21–28.

a. What does God promise them both?

_____

_____

b. What does God ask of Abraham? What does Hannah know she must do?

_____

_____

c. Read James 2:21–22. What was God really seeking when he asked Abraham to make such a sacrifice?

_____

_____

_____

d. Why was Hannah willing to make her sacrifice?

_____

_____

e. Have you ever been asked to give back something that was precious to you? How did you respond?

_____

_____

_____

f. What can we learn from Abraham and Hannah about what our own attitudes should be towards the sacrifices we're called to make?

_____

_____

_____

"But what does it all mean?" asked Susan when they were somewhat calmer.

"It means that though the witch knew the Deep Magic, there is deeper magic still which she did not know. Her knowledge goes back only to the dawn of time. But if she could have looked a little further back, into the stillness and the darkness before Time dawned, she would have read there a different incantation. She would have known that when a willing victim who committed no treachery was killed in a traitor's stead, the Table would crack and Death itself would start working backward."[1]

C. S. Lewis

4. Although the Israelites made a great many sacrifices to God, He wasn't pleased with all of those sacrifices. Read the following passages and then answer the questions below.

Genesis 4:3–5
Amos 5:21–24
Malachi 1:6–9
Hebrews 11:4

a. What types of sacrifice are not pleasing to God? What makes for a pleasing sacrifice?

_____

_____

b. Have you ever made a sacrifice with the wrong attitude? What were the consequences?

_____

_____

[1] C. S. Lewis, *The Lion, the Witch, and the Wardrobe*, 1950 (New York: First Harper Trophy Edition, 1994), 163.

5. The animal sacrifices weren't ultimately what God was after. He was after something deeper, something that He still wants from us today—love and obedience. So what, according to Hebrews 10:1–5, was the point of God asking Israel to make so many animal sacrifices to Him?

_____

_____

6. According to Hebrews 10:12–18, what is the one sacrifice that was efficacious?

_____

_____

> Outward sacrifice, to be genuine, must be the expression of spiritual sacrifice. . . . The prophets of the Old Covenant often denounced sacrifices that were not from the heart or not coupled with love of neighbor. . . . The only perfect sacrifice is the one that Christ offered on the cross as a total offering to the Father's love and for our salvation. By uniting ourselves with his sacrifice we can make our lives a sacrifice to God.
>
> Catechism, no. 2100

7. Although Christ's sacrifice has opened the way for us to eternal life, why, as the following Scripture passages tell us, should we continue to make sacrifices? What do our sacrifices merit?

Colossians 1:24
Romans 5:1–5
Philippians 1:29

_____

_____

8. Read Romans 12:1–2.

a. What does it mean to offer our bodies as a living sacrifice?

_____

_____

b. In what ways have you offered your body as a living sacrifice?

_____

_____

9. Can you practice courageous generosity without sacrifice? Why or why not?

_____

_____

10. How does the world's understanding of sacrifice differ from the understanding of sacrifice we receive from Scripture?

_____

_____

11. Reflecting on your own life and what you've learned in this lesson, answer the following questions:

a. Is there any sacrifice that God is asking you to make right now that you haven't made?

_____

b. Based upon the Scriptures you've just read, what are some ways you can overcome the obstacles preventing you from making that sacrifice?

_____

_____

c. What are some of the small daily sacrifices you can make that will help those you love, help you grow closer to God, and help prepare you for the bigger sacrifices God is calling you or may call you to make?

_____

_____

Memory Verse

*"I appeal to you therefore, brethren,
by the mercies of God, to present
your bodies as a living sacrifice, holy
and acceptable to God, which is
your spiritual worship."*
Romans 12:1

Prayer:
The Fuel of Generosity

Recently, I came across one of those studies that chronicles what Americans believe about God. One statistic stood out in particular. It said that nearly three-quarters of Americans pray at least once a week.[1] My reactions to that little fact were mixed.

On the one hand, I thought, it's great that so many people are talking to God. But on the other hand, what kind of conversation can they be having if they're only talking once a week?

Don't get me wrong. Some prayer is definitely better than no prayer. Yet, if I told you that I only spoke with my husband once a week, what would you think about our marriage? I'm guessing you would have your doubts about the strength and closeness of our relationship. And you would be perfectly right to have those doubts. No marriage could ever survive, let alone thrive, if a husband and wife only had brief chats once a week. Similarly, no relationship with God can sustain us or transform us if we only go to Him once every seven days.

Prayer is the means by which we build a relationship with God. Sure, He knows what we're thinking without us having to tell Him. But He wants us to tell Him nonetheless. He wants us to turn to Him not just once a week, or even once a day, but repeatedly throughout the day. That's why the Bible admonishes us to "pray constantly," and to "continue steadfastly in prayer, being watchful in it with thanksgiving" (Col. 4:2).

---

[1] Charles Chaput, *Render unto Caesar: Serving the Nation by Living Our Catholic Beliefs in Political Life* (New York: Doubleday, 2008), 31.

God doesn't want us to pray like that because *He* needs it.
He wants it because *we* need it. We need to go to Him constantly, repeatedly, again and again so that we can learn to hear
His voice speaking to us and see His hand guiding us. We need
to go to Him so that we can both be transformed by Him and
receive the grace we need to live the lives He calls us to lead.
"Jesus, I want to see your face," is the prayer of the heart longing for its Savior.

Without prayer, courageous generosity is just a pipe dream,
a pleasant but unrealistic thought. This chapter is about why
that is the case.

1. If we're not praying as we ought, it might be because we don't
have a clear understanding of the nature of prayer. According
to the Catechism, nos. 2559 and 2565, what is prayer?

_____

_____

2. Humility is the virtue whereby we have an accurate self-
knowledge or "self-image." Humility informs us that *apart from
Jesus* we are nothing and can do nothing of value. It instructs
us that *in Him* we are precious daughters of the King of heaven
who have all we need and are empowered to do His work on
earth. All that is good in us comes from His divine goodness
and all our failings can be overcome through His mighty grace.[2]
We are blessed indeed!

a. Humility is the basis of prayer. Why?

_____

_____

---

[2] Extension activity: Look up James 1:17–18, 1 Corinthians 1:26–31, Ephesians
2:1–10 to see some biblical explanations of these truths.

b. What does God promise to the humble in 2 Chronicles 7:14–15? _____

_____

c. Sometimes we fail in humility when we give in to pride. But we also can fail in humility by practicing false humility. Can you think of an example of false humility? How does this hinder our relationship with God?

_____

_____

> "Souls without prayer are like people whose bodies or limbs are paralyzed: They possess feet and hands, but they cannot control them."[3]
>
> St. Teresa of Avilla

Prayer requires more than humility. It also requires faith. Faith, according to Hebrews 11:1, is "the assurance of things hoped for, the conviction of things not seen." Faith is the virtue that enables us to believe the truth of God even though we cannot physically see Him. We accept this truth based on the testimony and trustworthiness of God Himself.[4] St. Peter tells it this way in 1 Peter 1:8–9, "Without having seen him you love him; though you do not now see him you believe in him and rejoice with unutterable and exalted joy. As the outcome of your faith you obtain the salvation of your souls."

---

[3] St. Teresa of Avilla, *Interior Castle* (New York: Doubleday, 1989), 31.
[4] An apologetic note: We accept many things on faith on much less than the testimony of God Himself. For example, most believe that a planet called Jupiter exists. How do we know this? Scientists tell us that it is true and we believe them.

3. What do you think James 5:13–14 is saying to us about the connection between prayer and faith?

_____

_____

4. Read David's prayer in Psalm 62:5–8. How does this prayer reflect a connection between humility, faith, and prayer?

_____

_____

5. What does Jesus tell us is the effect of prayers offered in faith? See Matthew 21:22.

_____

_____

6. Scripture tells of five forms of prayer. What type of prayer do the following verses describe? Describe the prayer form in your own words.

Reference Verses	Prayer Form
Luke 1:62–64 Luke 2:25–35 Psalm 103:1–5	
1 John 3:21–22 1 John 1:8–10 James 1:5–8 Philippians 4:6–7	
Numbers 14:13–20 James 5:16 Colossians 4:12 Romans 8:26	

1 Thessalonians 5:18 Romans 8:16 2 Corinthians 2:14 Psalm 118:1	
Ephesians 1:3 Revelation 5:11–14 Psalm 100 Psalm 98 Psalm 113	

Prayer is both a gift of grace and a determined response on our part. It always presupposes effort. The great figures of prayer of the Old Covenant before Christ, as well as the Mother of God, the saints, and he himself, all teach us this: *prayer is a battle.* Against whom? Against ourselves and against the wiles of the tempter who does all he can to turn man away from prayer, away from union with God. We pray as we live, because we live as we pray. If we do not want to act habitually according to the Spirit of Christ, neither can we pray habitually in his name. *The "spiritual battle" of the Christian's new life is inseparable from the battle of prayer.*

Catechism, no. 2725 (emphasis added)

7. Spiritual warfare is real and the battle between God and the devil for our souls extends to our prayer life as much as the rest of our life. We are tempted in so many ways to neglect, give up, or not even try in our prayer lives.

a. What are some of the temptations that keep you from prayer and that prevent you from going deeper in prayer?

_____

_____

b. What is our *real* problem when we allow these temptations to conquer our will to pray?

_____

_____

c. What needs to be our response to these temptations?

_____

_____

8. Mary, Martha, and their brother Lazarus, whom Jesus raised from dead, were dear friends of Jesus. In a memorable encounter between the two women and Jesus, we are taught about right priorities. Read Luke 10:38–41.

a. What were Martha's priorities and what was wrong with them in these circumstances?

_____

_____

b. What was Mary's priority?

_____

_____

c. Do you ever find yourself acting more like Martha when you should be acting more like Mary? Give an example.

_____

_____

d. How can you apply the lesson Jesus teaches to Martha to your own life?

_____

_____

9. Prayer must be the beginning of any act of generosity. If we are not turning to God in prayer—seeking His will, His strength, His grace—any effort at generosity elsewhere will fall flat. Our efforts will be disconnected from their source of goodness. They will be rooted in our strength, not His. Can you think of any times you tried to practice generosity without relying on God in prayer? What were the results?

_____

_____

_____

_____

"Necessity obliges us to pray for ourselves. Fraternal charity obliges us to pray for others. God finds the prayer motivated by charity more meritorious than the prayer motivated by necessity."

St. Bernard, "Sermon on the Assumption of the
Blessed Virgin Mary"

10. Our lives are so busy and seemingly busier by the day.

a. How, with all the demands on your time and energy, have you found time to prioritize prayer?

_____

_____

_____

b. In what way does this take courage?

_____

_____

_____

c. Can you think of two things you can start doing immediately that will help you be more generous with God in prayer?

_____

_____

Memory Verse

"Have no anxiety about anything, but in
everything by prayer and supplication with
thanksgiving let your requests be made
known to God. And the peace of God,
which passes all understanding, will keep
your hearts and your minds in Christ Jesus."
Philippians 4:6–7

Family Life, Part I:
"Till Death Do Us Part"—
Our Relationship with Our Spouse

A Christian marriage is probably the most wonderful and difficult relationship a person can ever have. I've learned this from my own experience. When my husband and I were first married, we were fairly wide-eyed and naive. We were in love and full of hopes and dreams. Then the honeymoon was over. That meant graduate school for him, a new teaching job for me, and a whole lot of stress for both of us. Soon came a new baby, a new job, and a new town. It was no longer all roses and sunshine.

Yes, we were in love. But we were also very selfish. There was the ideal we believed—both the theological ideal given to us by our faith and the romantic ideal—and then there was reality— the baby, the almost empty checking account, the differences in opinion over the grocery list, and all the other bits of marital life they don't show you in the movies.

Since then, like most, we have had our share of sickness and health, good times and bad, plenty and want. Together through the years, we've endured struggles much more painful than the stress of a new job and tight finances. We've also shared joys much greater than new jobs or new houses. We've clung tightly to the Church's teaching on marriage, claiming the grace of the Sacrament again and again.

Slowly, very slowly, through this Sacrament, we grow a little less selfish each year. Bit by bit, we've learned, however imperfectly and inconsistently, to defer to the other out of love for Christ. And we know that this slow and steady path of self-renunciation and self-gift is the path God has laid for us to find our way to our eternal home.

Our path is also very much like the path trod by all married couples, including Adam and Eve.

1. In the Book of Genesis, we learn that marriage is an institution created by God, "in the beginning." While familiar, the story of the first marriage is foundational to a proper understanding of the nature of marriage. It is worth revisiting these oft quoted verses. By the way, the Book of Genesis contains two consecutive stories of the Creation. The first is a brief overview that contains the order and days of Creation. The second is a fuller explanation of the Garden of Eden and the "creation of man."

a. Read Genesis 1:26–28. In Genesis 1:26, it says, "Let us make man in our image, after our likeness." What does it mean to be made in the image of God? For the Church's explanation, please read *Catechism of the Catholic Church*, nos. 356–368.

_____

_____

_____

You will notice that being made in the image of God means that each of us possesses the ability to freely give ourself to another. When we do that, we imitate the persons of the Blessed Trinity, who give themselves to each other, fully and freely, in love. The ability to give ourselves is a gift of God. The love that flows in a marriage is to resemble and image the love that flows in the Trinity.

b. In Genesis 1:28 what three things does God command man and woman to do? Use your own words to explain the meaning of each.

1. _____

2. _____

3. _____

2. Read Genesis 2:18–25. Verse 18 demonstrates the fatherly love and concern of our heavenly Father for His beloved children. What is the problem God observes and what does it teach us about human nature?

_____

_____

3. In verse 18, God's solution is, "I will make a helper fit for him."

a. What is a helper?

_____

b. What does it mean that this creature is to be "fit for him?"

_____

_____

4. The "helper fit for him" is God's description of the interpersonal relationship of the couple. This design is repeated again and again with each couple that God has joined in Holy Matrimony. If you are married, this design has been repeated in your own marriage, too.

a. How is your spouse "fit" for you and you for him?

_____

_____

b. How has this "fit" made it possible for you to help each other?

_____

c. Are there any practical ways that you can seek to be a better helpmate to your spouse right now?

_____

_____

_____

5. In verse 24 we read, "Therefore a man *leaves* his father and his mother and *cleaves* to his wife, and they become one flesh." In light of this entire reading (Gen. 2:18–25), what does it mean to "leave and cleave" and why is it done?

_____

_____

> The matrimonial covenant, by which a man and a woman establish between themselves a partnership of the whole of life, is by its nature ordered toward the good of the spouses and the procreation and education of offspring; this covenant between baptized persons has been raised by Christ the Lord to the dignity of a sacrament.
> Catechism, no. 1601, quoting Code of Canon Law, can. 1055 §1

6. Read the Catechism, nos. 1604–1605. You will notice that it echoes the Genesis passages we just studied. According to the Catechism, what is the mission of married love?

_____

_____

"Finally, Christian spouses, in virtue of the sacrament of Matrimony, whereby they signify and partake of the mystery of that unity and fruitful love which exists between Christ and His Church, help each other to attain to holiness in their married life and in the rearing and education of their children. By reason of their state and rank in life they have their own special gift among the people of God. From the wedlock of Christians there comes the family, in which new citizens of human society are born, who by the grace of the Holy Spirit received in baptism are made children of God, thus perpetuating the people of God through the centuries. The family is, so to speak, the domestic church. In it parents should, by their word and example, be the first preachers of the faith to their children; they should encourage them in the vocation which is proper to each of them, fostering with special care vocation to a sacred state."

Second Vatican Council, Dogmatic Constitution on
the Church *Lumen Gentium*, no. 11

7. Because marriage was part of God's plan from the beginning, present even before the Fall, the Church refers to marriage as "the primordial sacrament." With the coming of Christ, it was given an added dignity as an image of Christ's relationship to the Church and as one of the seven sacraments in the Church. As a sacrament, marriage becomes a means of sanctifying grace for those called to it. It is our school of love and path to holiness. St. Paul gives wise words for the married in Ephesians 5:21–33. Read this passage and then answer the following questions.

St. Paul tells us that we are to "be subject to one another out of reverence for Christ." Pope John Paul II called this a "mutual subjection" of the spouses.[1]

a. What does it mean to be mutually subject to one another, and how is this an extension of God's design for the spouses to be help mates?

_____

_____

b. How is mutual subjection a school of love and a path to holiness?

_____

_____

c. Why is it so hard?

_____

_____

8. There are many forces at work in us and in our world that threaten to destroy our marriages. Sins against the sixth commandment, "Thou shall not commit adultery," including both adultery and divorce, are grave offenses against marriage.[2] But adultery and divorce do not happen instantaneously and in a void. It is usually the end result of a long process that includes offenses against the dignities of each person. Many of these offenses are rooted in lust, and those sins begin in the heart, not the flesh. As Jesus warned, "every one who looks at a woman lustfully has already committed adultery with her in his heart" (Mt. 5:28). Today, one of the most wide-spread and per-

---

[1] John Paul II, Apostolic Letter *Mulieris Dignitatem* (August 15, 1988), no. 24 (Boston: St. Paul Books and Media, 1988), 83.

[2] See Matthew 19:3–12, and Catechism, "Offenses against the Dignity of Marriage," nos. 2380–2391.

vasive of these attacks, an attack which violates the dignity of the human person and the sanctity of marriage, is the proliferation of pornography. Pornography, in any and all forms—from immodest and suggestive magazine covers, to commercials and news headlines, to the extreme ends of human depravity—reduce people to objects and undermine their dignity as created images of God. They also pervert the legitimate and beautiful expression of human love meant to unfold in the context of the permanent and indissoluble bond of marriage. As the woman of the home, you can help protect the chastity of your marriage, your sons' and husband's purity, and teach your daughters the dignity of their persons. What are some practical ways that you can do this?

_____

_____

> "By matrimony, therefore, the souls of the contracting parties are joined and knit together more directly and more intimately than are their bodies, and that not by any passing affection of sense or spirit, but by a deliberate and firm act of the will; and from this union of souls by God's decree, a sacred and inviolable bond arises."[3]
>
> Pius XI

9. Many marriage counselors wisely advise couples that marriage is a 110%–110% deal. We are to give it all and more, if we expect to have a healthy, loving relationship. This is why it images the love of God—total love, total self-gift. We give until it hurts. We lay down our life for our friend or, in this case, spouse. We give when they've acted selfishly, when we are disappointed, angry (justly or not), or when we aren't sure this is what we bargained for. When we do this we experience

---

[3] Pope Pius XI, Encyclical Letter on Christian Marriage *Casti Connubii* (December 31, 1930) [Boston, MA: St. Paul Books and Media], 7.

the irony involved in the whole Gospel—we lose our life in order to take it up again.[4] We lay down our lives for our loved ones and then receive a love in return we could never have dreamed of—something much more meaningful and beautiful than ever has been portrayed in movies or a romance novel.

It requires that we believe with the Church that marriage is indissoluble—that God has united you with your spouse and this marriage is bigger than just the two of you. Your marriage is worth fighting for because it is your path to holiness.

(a) Can you recall a particular instance when you have shown love to your spouse during a difficult time, when you didn't want to? What was the result? (b) What can you do for your spouse this week that will show him that you love him and are thankful that God has given him to you?

a. _____

_____

b. _____

_____

Memory Verse
"*Be subject to one another out
of reverence for Christ.*"
Ephesians 5:21

---

[4] Matthew 16:25.

Family Life, Part II:
The Gift of Children

When it comes to the virtues and the spiritual life, I've learned my most important lessons from the school of parenting. Daily, my children help me understand more deeply the kind of love that God is and gives. They stretch me to what I used to think were impossible levels of love, patience, suffering, and courage. And they remind me how much further I still need to grow.

My children also water the seeds of a deep and abiding love between my husband and me. They are the fruit of love that continues to bear the fruit of love. As we work to provide for them and educate them, laugh and pray with them, suffer with them, and simply walk with them through this life, my husband and I fall more and more deeply in love with each other.

Our experience isn't unique. Countless other couples have learned these same lessons and grown in love in these same ways. And that is because this is God's plan for married life. It's what He wants for every married couple in every generation.

"Will you accept children lovingly from God, and bring them up according to the law of Christ and his Church?"[1] Every Catholic couple married in the Roman rite of the Church must answer that question during their wedding ceremony, a question which hearkens back to God's command in Eden: "be fruitful and multiply" (Gen.1:28). The question is asked because children are a primary end of marriage and an integral part of the Sacrament. The Second Vatican Council, restating the perpetual teaching of the Church, proclaimed, "Marriage and conjugal love are by their nature ordained to the begetting and rearing of

---

[1] Pope John Paul II, Letter to Families from Pope John Paul II: 1994 Year of the Family *Gratissimam Sane*, (February 2, 1994), no. 16, quoting *Rituale Romanum, Ordo Celebrandi Matrimonium*, n. 60, [Boston, MA: St. Paul Books and Media, 1994].

children. Indeed, children are the *most precious gift* of marriage
and *contribute immensely to the good of the parents* themselves."[2]

   Children do contribute much to the good of their parents.
They give us joy and laughter. They also give us the opportunity
to die to ourselves daily. They cost us our wants and sometimes
our needs and, in the process, they give us the chance to receive
innumerable spiritual gifts. It is here, in God's vision for marriage and family, that our faith is tested and our wills stretched.
It is here that virtues are acquired and the potential for holiness
realized. Making that vision our own and living it faithfully
requires nothing less than heroic generosity.

1. Each of the following verses discusses the sovereignty of God
in the procreation of children. What are the words used to
describe God's power over new life? What do they make clear
about children?

a. Genesis 21:1–2: _____

b. Genesis 30:1–2: _____

c. 1 Samuel 1:5: _____

d. Psalm 113:9: _____

2. In the following two passages Jesus interacts with children
and teaches us a lesson about both God and little ones. Read
each passage and answer:

a. How does Jesus treat children and what is His perspective
on their value?

---

[2] Second Vatican Council, Pastoral Constitution on the Church in the Modern
World *Gaudium et Spes*, no. 50, emphasis added.

b. How does Jesus use children to teach us a lesson about God and the Christian life? What is the lesson?

Matthew 19:13–15

a. _____

b. _____

Mark 9:35–37

a. _____

b. _____

> "That a new human being should issue from it [the marital act] is certainly part of the solemn grandeur of this supremely intimate union. The wonderful, divinely-appointed relationship between the mysterious procreation of a new human being and this most intimate communion of love (which by itself alone already has its full importance), illuminates the grandeur and solemnity of this union."[3]
>
> Dietrich Von Hildebrand

3. Use Psalm 127:3–5 and Psalm 128:3–4 to answer the following.

a. According to Psalm 127:3, what are children? _____

_____

b. What is the general lesson being taught by both of these passages?_____

_____

---

[3] Dietrich Von Hildebrand, Marriage, *The Mystery of Faithful Love* (Manchester, NH: Sophia Institute Press, 1997), 27.

4. Read the Catechism, no. 2378.

a. According to this passage, what is a child? _____

_____

b. What rights does the child have?_____

_____

"Every human being is always to be accepted as a gift and blessing of God."[4] This is the lesson of both Testaments of Scripture and the Church's teaching from its very beginnings. The Church has consistently stood on the side of life because God is the Author of life.

But today, we can't speak about children without also speaking about artificial birth control. For many, particularly women, this isn't an easy conversation. Some of us have been misled by the culture, which says all responsible adults use birth control. Others of us are confused or unsure about what the Church teaches. For all of us, it is a deeply personal and, accordingly, deeply sensitive subject.

The Church's teaching, however, is clear. Artificial methods of birth control—both chemical methods and barrier methods—are gravely sinful because they violate the meaning of marital love and the dignity of the persons involved. The marital act, as instituted by God, is meant to be a complete gift of self to the other.[5] Its purpose is to unify the couple in love and to procreate children as the living embodiment of that love. Like the exchange of love within the Trinity, there is to be a total gift of self in the act. That means nothing is held back. When artificial birth control is used, however, something

---

[4] Congregation for the Doctrine of the Faith, Respect for Human Life *Donum Vitae* (February 22, 1987) [Boston, MA: St. Paul Books and Media, 1987], p. 23.
[5] Pope John Paul II, Letter to Families, no. 12.

is held back. Everything is not given. There is a barrier erected. God and the possibility of new life are shut out.

Up until 1930, all Christian denominations believed that and condemned the use of artificial birth control. It was not until August of 1930, at the Lambeth Conference, that the Anglican denomination first sanctioned its use. Pope Pius XI responded swiftly and firmly. In December of 1930 he issued the encyclical, *On Christian Marriage*. In it he taught:

> Since, therefore, the conjugal act is destined primarily by nature for the begetting of children, those who in exercising it deliberately frustrate its natural power and purpose sin against nature and commit a deed which is shameful and intrinsically vicious. . . . Since, therefore, openly departing from the uninterrupted Christian tradition some recently have judged it possible solemnly to declare another doctrine regarding this question, the Catholic Church, to whom God has entrusted the defense of the integrity and purity of morals, standing erect in the midst of the moral ruin which surrounds her. . . . our mouth proclaims anew: any use whatsoever of matrimony exercised in such a way that the act is deliberately frustrated in its natural power to generate life is an offense against the law of God and of nature, and those who indulge in such are branded with the guilt of a grave sin.[6]

Despite the Pope's statement, the use of contraception spread among Protestants and questions continued among Catholics. In the mid-60s, Pope Paul VI convened a special commission to address the question. Rumors began to spread

---

[6] Pius XI, On Christian Marriage *Casti Connubii*, St. Paul Books and Media edition, p. 28–29.

that the Church would follow the path taken by Protestant communities and sanction artificial birth control. As the rumors spread, Catholic couples, often following the counsel of their parish priest, began to contracept. But in 1968, Pope Paul VI ended those rumors with his encyclical letter, *On the Regulation of Birth*, also known by its Latin name, *Humanae Vitae*. In it he wrote:

> In conformity with these fundamental elements of the human and Christian vision of marriage, we must once again declare that the direct interruption of the generative process already begun, and, above all, directly willed and procured abortion, even if for therapeutic reasons, are to be absolutely excluded as lawful means of birth regulation.
>
> Also, to be excluded, as the Magisterium of the Church has on a number of occasions declared, is direct sterilization, whether perpetual or temporary, whether of the man or of the woman.
>
> Similarly excluded is every action that, either in anticipation of the conjugal act or in its accomplishment or in the development of its natural consequences, would have as an end or as a means, to render procreation impossible.[7]

Although many Catholics have rejected the Church's teaching against artificial birth control, it remains as true and binding today as it was in 1968. Pope John Paul II reiterated that in several of his own encyclicals and letters, as have the United States Bishops.

On this subject, all of our shepherds are echoing the teaching of Scripture.

---

[7] Pope Paul VI, Encyclical Letter On the Regulation of Births *Humanae Vitae* (July 25, 1968), no. 14 [San Francisco: Ignatius Press, 1968], p. 12.

5. In Genesis 38, we read the story of a man named Onan who was to marry the widow of his deceased older brother—the first born son of Judah. This was the tradition among the Jews and a means for protecting and providing for widows. In Jewish law, however, a child that would be conceived of this union would still be considered an heir of the first born son and thus the heir of Judah. Read Genesis 38:8–10. What did Onan do that warranted God's punishment?

_____

_____

6. The Catechism addresses the issue in nos. 2366–2367, 2370. Read these passages. Why does the Church teach that each marital act must remain open to new life?

_____

_____

"Thus, in the sexual relationship between man and woman two orders meet, which has as its object reproduction, and the personal order which finds its expression in the love of persons and aims at the fullest realization of that love. We cannot separate the two orders, for each depends upon the other. In particular, the correct attitude to procreation is a condition of the realization of love. . . . Sexual relations between a man and a woman in marriage have their full value as a union of persons only when they go with conscious acceptance of the possibility of parenthood."[8]

Pope John Paul II

---

[8] John Paul II (Karol Wojtyla), *Love and Responsibility* (San Francisco: Ignatius Press, 1997), 226–227.

7. The Church, while recognizing "in large families a sign of God's blessing and the parents' generosity,"[9] does not teach that you must have as many children as you are physically able to conceive. Rather, it teaches that married couples should exercise responsible parenthood. Pope Paul VI in *Humanae Vitae* wrote: "In relation to physical, economic, psychological and social conditions, responsible parenthood is exercised either by the thoughtfully made and generous decision to raise a large family, or by the decision, made for grave motives and with respect for the moral law, to avoid a new birth for the time being, or even for an indeterminate period." And later, "If, then, there are serious motives for spacing births, motives deriving from the physical or psychological conditions of husband or wife, or from external circumstances, the Church teaches that it is then permissible to take into account the natural rhythms immanent in the generative functions and to make use of marriage during the infertile times only, and in this way to regulate births without offending the moral principles that we have just recalled."[10]

Also, read the Catechism, no. 2368.

Under what circumstances is it permissible to regulate births through what is now known as "natural family planning?"[11]

_____

_____

It is helpful to remember that, whatever circumstances may warrant the spacing of children, be it financial troubles,

---

[9] Catechism, no. 2373.
[10] Pope Paul VI, On the Regulation of Births, nos. 10 and 16.
[11] There are many sources to learn more about up-to-date natural family planning methods, including the Couple to Couple League (www.ccli.org, 800-745-8252) and the Pope Paul XVI Institute (www.popepaulvi.com, 402-390-6600). You can also contact the chancery in your own diocese for more information.

psychological stress, spousal difficulties, etc., God is ultimately the Author of life. The creation of a human person is not merely a biological process. Recall from the first question—it is God who opens or closes the womb, and it is God who infuses a soul. Ultimately, the creation of a new life is the will of God.

8. Although living these teachings often requires couples to face incredible challenges, it also brings wonderful blessings. What blessings have you been given in living this teaching? If you have not been living this teaching, what steps do you need to take to begin to do so?

_____

_____

9. Welcoming children is only the beginning of parenting. Educating them and forming them is our ultimate duty. According to the following passages, what it the primary educational goal of parents?

a. Deuteronomy 4:9–10

_____

b. Deuteronomy 32:44–46

_____

c. Psalm 78:1–8

_____

d. What are ways that we can go about implementing these goals?

_____

_____

10. As an important part of educating children, we must encourage them to discern their vocation, whether that be religious life, marriage, or single life. How can we guide them to be generous and responsive to God, no matter what their calling in life?

_____

_____

> "*Parents are the first and most important educators* of their own children, and they also possess a fundamental competence in this area: they are *educators because they are parents.* They share their educational mission with other individuals or institutions, such as the Church and the state. But the mission of education must always be carried out in accordance with a proper application of the *principle of subsidiary.*"[12]
>
> Pope John Paul II

11. Read Ephesians 6:4 and Colossians 3:21.

a. What advice does St. Paul offer parents in these following?

_____

_____

_____

b. How can we do this with both our young children and those who are grown?

_____

_____

[12] Pope John Paul II, Letter to Families, no. 16.

"It is above all in raising children that the family fulfulls its mission to proclaim the Gospel of life. By word and example, in the daily round of relations and choices, ad through concrete actions and signs, parents lead their children to authentic freedom. . . . In raising children Christian parents must be concerned about their children's faith and help them to fulfill the vocation God has given them."[13]

John Paul II

12. Living the teachings of the Church on children requires nothing less than courageous generosity. The Church herself acknowledges this repeatedly. There has been nothing in my life that has tested my faith or virtue more, but it is a powerful means to holiness if we will accept it. How can living the teachings of the Church on children lead us to holiness?

———————————————————————————————

———————————————————————————————

Memory Verse
"Whoever receives one such child in
my name receives me; and whoever
receives me, receives not me
but him who sent me."
Mark 9:37

---

[13] John Paul II, Encyclical Letter on the Gospel of Life *Evangelium Vitae* (March 25, 1995), no. 92 [Boston, MA: St. Paul Books and Media], p. 146, emphasis added.

Love Thy Neighbor

When am I most likely to fail to act on my resolutions to live generously? At about 5:00 p.m. That's when a pot is boiling over on the stove, a baby is crying, a toddler is standing on a chair ready to plunge headfirst to the floor, older children are clamoring for my attention, and the phone is ringing. On the other end of the phone? A man trying to sell me a satellite dish.

Being kind to that telemarketer takes heroic generosity. It actually takes super-heroic generosity. And I'll be honest, I don't always have it.

Every day, each of us is called to give of ourselves to friends, neighbors, and perfect strangers. From the friend who stops by with a question, to the checkout clerk at the grocery store, our day is an endless succession of opportunities to practice heroic generosity to all who cross our paths. Sometimes this is easy. Many times, it's not. Regardless, each encounter calls us outside of ourselves to see Jesus in each person and to love them as Jesus would have us do.

What a tremendous gift that is—to be able to love Jesus through our interactions with others. We can greet the image of God placed in their souls and love them as if each of them was Jesus Himself. Jesus recognizes that love as more than a sign of our love for Him. He recognizes it as our actual act of loving Him.

Because of that, loving our neighbor is a path to God. It leads us to Him and it leads us to holiness. Accordingly, it is important that we know how to do it.

1. The Gospels record Jesus telling his listeners the "Greatest Commandment." Read both Matthew 22:35–40 and Mark 12:28–34.[1]

a. Notice that the love of God and love of neighbor are connected. St. Matthew says, "a second is *like* it." How is the commandment to love your neighbor "*like*" the love of God?

_____

_____

b. The scribe that Jesus addresses in Mark's account replies that to love God and one's neighbor is "much more than all whole burnt offerings and sacrifices." The scribe is referring to the sin offerings required by Levitical law. Jesus responds by saying, "you are not far from the kingdom of God." Why is this man "not far from the kingdom of God?" Why do Christians still need to learn this lesson even when we no longer have a Levitical sacrificial system to obey?

_____

_____

2. a. According to Romans 13:8–10, Galatians 5:13–14, and James 2:8 what are we doing when we love our neighbor?

_____

_____

_____

b. According to Matthew 5:17–20, why is this important?

_____

_____

---

[1] There is another account of this in Luke 10:25–28.

3. St. John tells us, "Beloved, if God so loved us, we also ought to love one another. No man has ever seen God; if we love one another, God abides in us and *his love is perfected in us*" (1 Jn. 4:11–12, emphasis added). In other words, if we truly love one another, we live the life of God in us and become holy. Loving our neighbor is intimately connected with our path to God—it *is* our path to God!

a. Read John 15:12–14, 17. According to Jesus, how do we love your neighbor?

_____

_____

b. What does this mean?

_____

_____

Working for Our Neighbor

We know we're supposed to love our neighbor, but how do we do that? What does it entail? And how can we actively and generously love our neighbors while living our own busy lives? The pages of the Bible are filled with stories of men and women who show us the answers to these questions. And of all those men and women, nobody did it better than Jesus and our Mother Mary. Let's look to the example they set for some basic principles we can apply to our own lives.

4. When the Angel Gabriel is speaking to Mary he reveals that her aged cousin Elizabeth is with child. Mary makes the long journey from Nazareth to Judah to visit her cousin. Read Luke 1:36–40.

a. What is Mary's condition when she is going to visit Elizabeth?

_____

b. How does she travel?

_____

c. What can we presume is the purpose of her visit?

_____

d. What can we learn about loving our neighbor from this episode?

_____

5. The wedding at Cana is the first miracle of Jesus. It is also a lesson given to us by our Mother Mary on how to love our neighbor. Read John 2:1–11.

a. What is Mary's activity at the wedding? How would she have noticed that they were low on wine?

_____

_____

b. Why did Mary care that the wine was running out? What was she trying to do for the couple?

_____

_____

c. What is the lesson we can learn about loving our neighbor from this episode?

_____

_____

6. The numerous stories of Jesus' miracles and parables illustrate how Our Lord consistently showed kindness, gentleness, mercy, and action to all who approached Him. Read John 4:3–26, the story of the Samaritan woman.

a. Look again at verse 3. How did Jesus feel?

_____

_____

b. What did Jesus do, despite his feelings?

_____

_____

c. What example has Jesus set for us in this portion of the story?

_____

_____

In the above stories, Mary or Jesus did three things that teach us how to love our neighbor. First, they *noticed that there was a need*. This required paying attention to those around them, listening to them, and seeing even the needs that went unspoken. It meant taking notice of those beyond themselves and their immediate family circle. Secondly, both Jesus and Mary *stepped out of their comfort zones*. It wasn't easy for Mary to travel all that way to care for Elizabeth or to risk others' thinking she was intruding in another's wedding. In the case of the Samaritan woman, Jesus had already spent the morning traveling and likely serving. He was exhausted. But He didn't let that stop Him from doing what the moment required. Finally, they *did something to remedy the need*. They took action. They did this without complaining, judging, or gossiping.

7. Our Lord and Our Lady's example motivate us to love our neighbor through authentic love and concern for others' needs. Try to think of someone you can serve this week. Maybe you could visit an elderly neighbor, make a meal for a new mom, or volunteer to babysit a busy mom's little ones for an afternoon. What other ideas do you have? What needs do you see among your friends and neighbors? What will you do this week?

_____

_____

_____

"Stretch out your hand often by doing favors for your neighbor, by protecting from harm one who suffers under the weight of calumny; stretch out your hand to the poor man who begs from you; stretch out your hand to the Lord asking pardon for your sins. This is how you stretch out your hand, and this is how you will be cured."[2]

St. Ambrose of Milan

Responding to Our Neighbor

We can show the love of Christ to those around us by what we do for them, but also by the way we respond and interact with them.

8. Read Matthew 18:23–35 and then, Matthew 18:22. Explain the parable and the lesson Jesus is teaching to us.

_____

_____

9. Forgiving someone who has hurt us can be very difficult. It takes humility and a willingness to let go of our pride. It also

---

[2] St. Ambrose of Milan, Commentary on St. Luke's Gospel, cited in Francis Fernandez, In Conversation with God, vol. 4 (London: Scepter, 1997), 576.

means we have to remember that we are all sinners and that we are all broken at some level. Original sin has left its mark on each of us. Sometimes, however, our struggle isn't so much to forgive as it is another problem. Read Matthew 7:1–5.

a. Jesus admonishes us to banish a critical and proud spirit and attitude. Why do we fall into the sin of haughty attitude or judgment toward our neighbor? When we do this, what virtues are we lacking?

_____

_____

b. What can we do to overcome this temptation?

_____

_____

c. Is there any person or group with whom you struggle in this particular way? If so, what practical steps can you take to begin overcoming that struggle?

_____

_____

10. The Epistles are full of practical directions about how we should interact with our neighbors. Read the following passages. What does each teach us?

a. 1 Corinthians 13:1–7

_____

b. 1 Corinthians 12:12–26

_____

c. Ephesians 4:25–32

_____

d. Titus 3:1–7

_____

11. St. Ignatius of Loyola, summarizing the principles of St. Paul contained in the Scriptures,[3] gives practical guidance for following the command to think well of others and give them the benefit of the doubt. Here is his advice:

> Every good Christian ought to be more ready to give a favorable interpretation to another's statement than to condemn it. But if he cannot do so, let him ask how the other understands it. And if the latter understands it badly, let the former correct him with love. If that does not suffice, let the Christian try all suitable ways to bring the other to a correct interpretation so that he may be saved.[4]

a. What are the steps of charity summarized by St. Ignatius?

1. _____

2. _____

3. _____

4. _____

b. Give an example of where you have used this method to success or could have used it?

_____

_____

------

[3] 2 Timothy 2:23–26 is one of many.
[4] Catechism, no. 2478.

12. While we show our love for Jesus by loving our neighbor, we must always keep our heart fixed on Jesus. Read John 21:20–22.

a. What is Jesus' message to Peter?

_____

_____

b. What is the lesson for us?

_____

_____

_____

Memory Verse
"So faith by itself, if it has
no works, is dead."
James 2:17

Work & Money

Where I live, a lot of people work in some fashion or another for the Church: some at a Catholic university, others for Catholic apostolates and non-profit organizations, still others for the diocese and local parishes. All of these people are giving generously to God through their work.

But so are lots of other people in the community, people whose jobs have nothing to do with Catholicism. That includes accountants, computer programmers, doctors, and just about every other profession you can think of. It also includes those who never set foot into an office but rather work for their families at home.

These people give to God by giving to others, by serving people and helping meet their needs. They also give to God simply by how they go about their work, by the spirit with which they do what they do. And they give to God by being good stewards of the money they earn through their work, spending money wisely and giving generously.

All of us, regardless of whether we work for the Church or for the private sector, in an office or at home, are called to work for God. We're also called to see our work as more than something we do for our own personal fulfillment and more than a means to an end (i.e. paying the bills, advancing in a career, improving our reputation in the community). We're called to see our work as an opportunity to grow in grace and virtue. We're called to see it as an expression of our fundamental human dignity. We're called to see it as an opportunity for heroic generosity.

Work

1. Read Genesis 1:28 and 2:15.

a. What instructions does God give to man in both of these verses?

_____

_____

b. Are these instructions given before or after Adam and Eve fell from grace?

_____

_____

c. What does that tell us about the original place of work in God's plan?

_____

_____

2. After Adam and Eve fall, God's original plan is altered somewhat. Read Genesis 3:17–19.

a. What is it about work that changes after the Fall?

_____

_____

b. Original sin, however, didn't entirely change the nature of work in God's plan. According to the *Catechism of the Catholic Church*, no. 307, even after the Fall, how do we image God in our daily work?

_____

_____

3. Read the Catechism, no. 2427.

a. How can our work become a "means of sanctification"?

_____

_____

b. In your own daily work, either inside or outside of the home, what are your most difficult tasks?

_____

_____

_____

c. What opportunities for self-denial do those tasks give you? How can you better take advantage of those opportunities to grow closer to Christ?

_____

_____

_____

"Work is part and parcel of man's life on earth. It involves effort, weariness, exhaustion: signs of the suffering and struggle which accompany human existence and which point to the reality of sin and the need for redemption. But in itself work is not a penalty or a curse or a punishment: those who speak of it that way have not understood sacred Scripture properly. . . . Work, all work, bears witness to the dignity of man, to his dominion over creation. It is an opportunity to develop one's personality. It is a bond of union with others, the way to support one's family, a means of aiding in the improvement of the society in which we live and in the progress of all humanity. For a Christian these horizons extend and grow wider. For work is a participation in the creative work of God. When he

created man and blessed him, he said: 'Be fruitful, multiply, fill the earth, and conquer it. Be masters of the fish of
the sea, the birds of heaven and all living animals on the
earth.' And, moreover, since Christ took it into his hands,
work has become for us a redeemed and redemptive reality.
Not only is it the background of man's life, it is a means
and path of holiness. It is something to be sanctified and
something which sanctifies."[1]

St. Jose Marie Escriva

4. 1 Corinthians 12:4–6 tells us that "there are varieties of
gifts but the same Spirit; and there are varieties of service, but
the same Lord; and there are varieties of working, but it is the
same God who inspires them all in every one." Read the rest of
chapter 12.

a. How is the Body of Christ built up through its members' different gifts and talents?

_____

_____

b. In your work, how do you serve the Body of Christ?

_____

_____

c. What gift or talent has God given you that could be put to
the service of the Body of Christ? What will you do?

_____

_____

[1] St. Jose Marie Escriva, *Christ Is Passing By* (New York: Scepter, 1974), 47.

"You must understand now more clearly that God is calling you to serve him 'in and from' the ordinary, material and secular activities of human life. He waits for us every day, in the laboratory, in the operating theatre, in the army barracks, in the university lecture room, in the factory, in the workshops, in the field, in the home, and in all the immense panorama of work. Understand this well: there is something holy, something divine hidden in the most ordinary situations, and it is up to each one of you to discover it."[2]

St. Jose Marie Escriva

5. Read the following passages.

Proverbs 12:24
Ecclesiastes 3:22
Sirach 19:1
Colossians 3:23–24

a. In your own words, describe what each has to say about how Christians are called to approach their daily work.

1. _____

2. _____

3. _____

4. _____

b. Mark 6:1–3 tells us that before beginning his public ministry, Jesus labored in Nazareth as a carpenter. What does Jesus' chosen profession tell us about his attitudes towards work?

_____

_____

---

[2] Escriva, *Friends of God*, 62, as quoted in Francis Fernandez, *In Conversation with God* (New York: Scepter, 1994), vol. 4, 187.

c. Reflecting on the above passages and on Christ's own example, what attitude towards work do you have the most trouble practicing? What action can you take to correct that?

_____

_____

_____

Money

My husband loves his work. He would continue to do it even if he weren't getting paid. Or rather, he would keep doing it in his spare time, on evenings and weekends. However, if the checks from his employer stopped coming in tomorrow, he would be out looking for a new job immediately. Like most of us, my husband works not just for the joy of it, but for the very practical end of earning the money our family needs.

Our family needs dollars to pay the electric bill, buy the enormous amount of groceries our children consume, replace our aging minivan, and help us purchase all those other practical necessities this earthly life requires. Love of money very well may be "the root of all evil," as Paul so famously writes in 1 Timothy 6:10, but money is also a necessary ingredient for survival in this world. Even religious orders with a vow of poverty still need to raise money to keep their buildings in good repair, feed their community, and help them perform their various works of mercy.

Because all of us need money, all of us also need to learn how to use money for its intended ends, without letting our need for it or, perhaps more accurately, our desire for it, consume us.

6. Read Ephesians 4:28 and 2 Thessalonians 3:8–12.

a. According to these passages, why do we earn money?

_____

_____

b. What other reasons does the *Catechism of the Catholic Church* give in no. 2402 for accumulating property?

_____

_____

7. According to Psalm 37:21 and Psalm 112:5 what does it mean to be a good steward of the money we earn?

_____

_____

8. Throughout the Bible, we are warned against "the love of money."

a. What do 1 Timothy 6:10 and Matthew 6:24 say are the dangers of that "love?"

_____

_____

b. Can you think of some examples of what a "love of money" looks like in today's world or in your own experience?

_____

_____

c. What kind of consequences have you seen resulting from the "love of money?"

_____

_____

9. Read the following passages:

Hebrews 13:5
Proverbs 11:28
1 Timothy 6:17
Luke 12:22–34

a. Where are many of us tempted to place our trust?

_____

b. Where should we place it instead?

_____

c. What reasons do the above passages give us for doing that?

_____

_____

10. With Abraham, we are given the first explicit example of tithing. Abraham offered to God a tenth of his victory spoils.[3] However, it is not until Numbers 18 that we read of God's direct instruction on the matter. Here the people are told to offer a tenth of their produce to the Levites who are in turn to give a tenth of what they have received from the laity to the Aaronic priests. Hereafter, the people of God were expected to offer a tenth of their yearly income. This custom was not always observed faithfully. The prophet Malachi rebuked the people heartily for their laxness. Read Malachi 3:7–12.

a. God tells the people that they are "robbing" Him in their "tithes and offerings." They are not giving the tenth required of them. While it is not explicitly stated, why do you think the people are failing to tithe?

_____

_____

b. In verse 10, God issues a challenge—"put me to the test"—and promises to "pour down for you an overflowing blessing." These are words of both encouragement and blessing. Why, do you think God asks the people to give a tenth of their earnings?

---
[3] Genesis 14:20

Does the God of the Universe need their money?

_____

_____

11. The Pharisees meticulously tithed. Malachi would not have had cause to rebuke them for "robbing" God materially. However, Jesus says, "Woe to you, scribes and Pharisees, hypocrites!"[4] Read the entire context of this dialogue in Matthew 23:23–24.

a. What is the Pharisees' problem?

_____

_____

b. According to Jesus and the negative example of the Pharisees, what needs to be our motive and the disposition of our hearts when we give?

_____

_____

> "The rich man who gives to the poor does not bestow alms but pays a debt."
>
> St. Ambrose of Milan

12. In his second letter to the people of Corinth, St. Paul addresses the faithful about their offerings to the Church. Read 2 Corinthians 9:6–12.

a. St. Paul says here, "God loves a cheerful giver." In the context of this passage, what is his point?

_____

_____

---

[4] Matthew 23:23.

b. What does this passage teach you about giving generously?

_____

_____

13. The Church teaches, as one of the five precepts of the Church, "that the faithful are obliged to assist with the material needs of the Church, each according to his own ability."[5] My husband and I, following the long tradition of the Church and the commandments of the Old Testament, have always offered at least a tenth of our earnings to the Church and charity. We do this because it is a practical way of demonstrating our love and trust in God, as well as our commitment to be heroically generous. Sometimes honoring that commitment is very difficult, but that what makes it heroic. What's easy, by its very nature, is not heroic.

Time to do a personal examination. Have you been as generous as you could be in your offerings to the Church and the poor? Have you given out of love for God and His people or out of servile obedience or grudgingly?

_____

_____

--- *Memory Verse* ---
"If then you have not been faithful in
the unrighteous mammon, who will
entrust to you the true riches?"
Luke 16:11

---

[5] Catechism, no. 2043. See, also, Code of Canon Law, no. 222.

Sharing the Gospel

As a college student, I spent a lot of time evangelizing. I talked about Jesus to my friends and classmates on campus, and I talked about Him to perfect strangers on a summer mission project, in housing projects, and just about every other place I could think of. I even talked about Him one Spring break in a biker bar! Those to whom I talked were atheists, Mormons, agnostics, members of Hare Krishna, fellow Christians, and just about every other religious persuasion you can imagine.

While all that talking can be intimidating and a bit scary at first, I quickly learned that people want to hear the Gospel. They yearn for Jesus and the peace that only He can bring. They feel a void, an emptiness. Something is missing from their life, and they know it. Most people try to fill that void with what the world tells them will make them happy—money, sex, and power. But what they soon find out is that none of those things quite do the trick. In fact, they only leave them feeling emptier. What these people have, what we all have, is a Christ-shaped hole in our hearts. And only He can fill it.

Often, when people hear the Gospel, they know immediately that this is what they've been longing for all along. As St. Augustine said, "Our hearts are restless until they rest in thee." I saw the truth of this in the eyes of those with whom I shared Jesus. Sometimes, of course, people run from Jesus. They don't want to hear what you want to share right then. But over time, words once spoken can sink in, take root in restless hearts, and finally fill that void.

That's why Jesus wants us to share the saving message of the Gospel with our friends, neighbors, and family. Because they want it. They need it. They can't live without it. And even when we don't see immediate fruits, that doesn't mean that seeds haven't been planted.

So, how do we go about sharing the Gospel? There are countless ways, more ways than we could ever list here. The important thing is to just do it. And as with every other aspect of our Christian life, this call to spread the Gospel requires courageous generosity.

> "In speaking of the apostolate, I shall begin with a strong statement: in order to be a fruitful apostle, begin by being a saint—a soul of love. The only fruitfulness is holiness."[1]
>
> Fr. Jean C.J. d'Elbée

1. Before Jesus' Ascension into heaven, He gave His apostles the "Great Commission." Read Matthew 28:18–20. What did Jesus command His disciples to do?

_____

Here, it's important to note that lay people are not the normal administers of the Sacrament of Baptism, although it is possible in necessary situations. Typically, the privilege of baptizing another is reserved for the priest or deacon of the parish welcoming the person into communion with God and the family of God. This doesn't mean, however, that we're not called to carry out the "Great Commission" given by Christ to His apostles in Matthew 28.

The Catechism of the Catholic Church, tells us that the Sacrament of Confirmation: "gives us a special strength of the Holy Spirit to spread and defend the faith by word and action as true witnesses of Christ, to confess the name of Christ boldly, and never to be ashamed of the Cross" (Catechism, no.1303).

---

[1] Fr. Jean C.J. d'Elbée, *I Believe in Love* (Manchester, NH: Sophia Institute Press, 2001), 164.

It goes on to say that, "This 'character' perfects the common priesthood of the faithful, received in Baptism, and 'the confirmed person receives the power to profess faith in Christ publically and as it were officially (*quasi ex officio*)'" (Catechism, no. 1305).

These passages make it clear that the sharing of the Gospel is not something reserved for only those who receive Holy Orders. All of the confirmed faithful are called and empowered to this great task!

2. As we read the Gospels, we see how Jesus was unstoppable. Once His ministry began, He never let up preaching, healing, and performing miracles. His compassion and mercy were inexhaustible. Can you imagine how the God of the universe felt being confined to the human limitations He put upon Himself, seeing all the misery about Him, and wanting to do more than was possible within these human confines? He must have experienced the same sense of frustration we feel in the face of so much need. He truly can relate to our struggles. And that's why the example He gives us in Matthew 9:35–38 is so helpful. Read that passage and answer the following questions.

a. What was Jesus' response to the crowds?

_____

_____

b. What does Jesus tell His disciples to do to remedy the problem He saw?

_____

_____

c. What is the message to us?

_____

"Lay people, whose particular vocation places them in the midst of the world and in charge of the most varied temporal tasks, must for this very reason exercise a very special form of evangelization. Their primary and immediate task is not to establish and develop the ecclesial community—this is the specific role of the pastors—but to put to use every Christian and evangelical possibility latent but already present and active in the affairs of the world. Their own field of evangelizing activity is the vast and complicated world of politics, society, and economics, but also the world of culture, of the sciences and the arts, of international life, of the mass media. It also includes other realities which are open to evangelization, such as human love, the family, the education of children and adolescents, professional work, suffering. The more Gospel-inspired lay people there are engaged in these realities, clearly involved in them, competent to promote them and conscious that they must exercise to the full their Christian powers which are often buried and suffocated, the more these realities will be at the service of the kingdom of God and therefore of salvation in Jesus Christ, without in any way losing or sacrificing their human content but rather pointing to a transcendent dimension which is often disregarded."[2]

Pope Paul VI

---

[2] Pope Paul VI, Apostolic Exhortation *Evangelii Nuntiandi* (December 8, 1975), no. 70.

3. Jesus was constantly ministering to the people. But what people? To whom did he minister? What was the message? Using the Bible passages given in the first column, complete the table below.

Passage	Who is Jesus helping?	What is their position in society?	Who is a modern parallel?	What is Jesus' message?
John 3:1–15				
John 4:6–26				
John 7:37–44				
Matthew 9:9–13				

4. Throughout His time on earth, Jesus revealed Himself to people in many different ways. After reading each of the following Scripture passages, list how Jesus communicated the truth about Himself to the people.

a. Matthew 9:27–31

_____

b. Matthew 14:13–21

_____

c. Luke 5:1–11

_____

d. Luke 4:16–22

_____

e. Luke 19:1–8

_____

5. When it comes to preaching the Gospel, Jesus has given us His example to follow. According to your answers to questions 3 and 4 above:

a. To whom is the Gospel to be preached?

_____

_____

b. What is the message?

_____

_____

c. How, in imitation of Him, can we communicate that message?

_____

d. What do you think enabled Jesus to preach that message so clearly? What can we learn from that about making our own preaching more effective?

_____

_____

"Preach the Gospel always. When necessary, use words."
St. Francis of Assisi

6. We know the message of Jesus needs to be shared with everyone, and we know what that message is. But what should motivate us to spread the Good News? While this may be obvious, look at the following verses and answer what each says is our motivation for sharing Jesus?

a. Romans 10:14–17

_____

b. 1 Corinthians 9:16

_____

c. 1 Thessalonians 2:2–4

_____

d. 1 Thessalonians 3:2

e. Romans 1:16

"We are accused of separating ourselves from the popular masses of the state, which is false, because the Christian knows he is in the same boat as his fellow citizens, ship-mates in a common earthly destiny."[3]

Tertullian

7. When we preach Christ, the first fruit we're aiming for is belief. We seek to bring people to faith in Christ and His Church. But that is not the only fruit. More is expected of Christians than belief. We're all called to ongoing conversion, as is the culture. The Gospel has to become a part of every area of our life and every area of the culture.

What do the following verses say about ongoing conversion and the evangelization of the culture?

a. Romans 12:2–21

b. Romans 15:1–7

c. Matthew 5:14–17

d. Philippians 4:4–9

---

[3] Tertullian, *Apologetics*, 28, cited in Francis Fernandez, *Conversation with God, vol. 4* (London: Scepter, 1997), 354.

8. Are there any areas of your life where you have shut the door to the Gospel? Areas where you are not willing to be converted? If so, how do you think this compromises your ability to share the Gospel with others?

_____

_____

9. Think back to your own conversion.

a. Who were the witnesses that helped you come to believe in Christ?

_____

_____

b. What made their witness so powerful and effective?

_____

_____

c. What lessons can you draw from your own experience of conversion in speaking to others about Christ?

_____

_____

10. While we each are called to share Christ with the world, we all are not called to be preachers, teachers, or fulltime missionaries. As we read in another chapter, we are each part of the Body of Christ and we each have our own God-given gifts to offer to the Church and the world. What work are you doing to spread the Kingdom of God?

_____

11. What gifts have you been given that can help you preach Christ? How can you better use these gifts in the service of the Church?

_____

_____

Memory Verse
"Preach the word, be urgent in season
and out of season, convince, rebuke, and
exhort, be unfailing in patience and in teaching."

ANSWER KEY

Lesson 1:
Courageous Generosity

1.

a. Joshua was to lead the Israelites into the Promised Land and reclaim it for the Israelites.

b. This was a dangerous and daunting task. They were going into battle with the odds against them. The land was inhabited by a race of fierce warriors, and they would face a well-armed and well-fortified enemy.

c. "I will not fail you or forsake you."

d. Take time to reflect and, if you are in a study group, prepare to share your experience.

2.

a. Slavery.

b. Fear prevents us from doing what we should do. It intimidates, limits, and can even immobilize us. It can truly be a form of slavery.

c. Take time to relect and, if you are in a study group, prepare to share your experience.

3.

a. Judas betrayed Him, and the other apostles fled and denied Christ in His hour of need.

b and c. Take time to reflect and, if you are in a study group, prepare to share your thoughts and opinions.

4. Sin and selfishness are the sources of bondage. Christ's death on the cross and our new life in Him are the sources of our freedom.

5. God loves us enough to have even the hairs of our head numbered. He is intimately involved in our lives. He is a loving Father and, with Him in control, we have nothing to fear.

6. We are told in this passage that we have received a spirit of sonship. We are children of God and therefore free from the slavery of sin and fear.

7. Take time to reflect and, if you are in a study group, prepare to share your thoughts.

8.
- a. We are to give freely and abundantly of our time, our energy, our prayers, and our love; to practice patience; to endure sufferings; to imitate Christ.
- b. They all require self-sacrifice, dying to self, and putting on Christ.

9.
- a. Prosperity; you will get back what you give.
- b. Blessings.

10. Answers will vary but can include God becoming man—His infancy, serving when tired, associating with the outcasts of the world, giving Himself in the Eucharist, suffering for our sins, welcoming the Gentiles into His Kingdom, etc.

11. We are fallen creatures who suffer from concupiscence and must fight against our selfish tendencies. Allow women time to share their own fears and struggles with generosity.

Lesson 2:
Sacrifice: The Way to Joy

1.
a. God sacrifices animals from the Garden of Eden.
b. Literally, the sacrifice was made to give Adam and Eve animal skins with which they could cover their nakedness. Figuratively, it covered over their sin.
c. Sacrifices atone for sin.
d. Take time to reflect and, if you are in a study group, prepare to share your story.

2.
a. He would deliver Noah and his family from the flood that will destroy the rest of the human race.
b. He was to bring seven pairs of clean animals, a pair of all the unclean animals, and seven pairs of the birds of the air.
c. Noah built an altar and sacrificed a pair of every clean animal and a pair of every clean bird. The Lord was pleased by the sacrifice and promised never to entirely destroy the human race again. The fact that God told Noah to bring seven pairs of each of the "clean" animals, which means animals acceptable for sacrifice, and seven pairs of each of the birds, but only one pair of each of the "unclean" animals (animals not acceptable for sacrifice) means God was planning on Noah offering sacrifices of thanksgiving after the flood was over.
d. This reminds Noah and his family that their deliverance was a gift and came at a cost.
e. Take time to reflect and, if you are in a study group, prepare to share your thoughts.

3.

   a. Sons.

   b. Abraham is to sacrifice his son Isaac. Hannah must give her son to the Lord.

   c. He wanted Abraham to be willing to make the sacrifice as a demonstration of his faith in God and his trust in God's promise.

   d. Hannah was willing because she recognized that her son was a gift from the Lord and that he belonged to God, not her.

   e and f. Take time to reflect and, if you are in a study group, prepare to share your stories and thoughts.

4.

   a. God is not pleased with sacrifices when those making them are not righteous and don't practice justice, mercy, or compassion. A pleasing sacrifice is when we offer God the best we have in faith; when our sacrifices are an expression of love, not an attempt to bargain with God; and when the way we live our lives is also an expression of that love.

   b. Take time to reflect and, if you are in a study group, prepare to share your experience.

5. God required them to make so many sacrifices as a way of perpetually reminding them of their sinfulness and helping them understand that their efforts alone could never undo the consequences of the Fall.

6. Christ's offering of Himself on Calvary and the continuation of that offering before God in heaven.

7. We should continue to make sacrifices in imitation of Christ, as reparation for our sins, to produce character and faith, and to build up the body of Christ. Our sufferings merit grace for those for whom we suffer, as well as grace for us. They connect us more intimately to Christ's sufferings in His sacrifice, and they help make up for the suffering of sin.

8.

    a.   To give ourselves to God, His plan, and His ways, not to our own selfish desires or the ways of the world.

    b.   Take time to reflect and, if you are in a study group, prepare to share your story. Sacrifices can be childbirth, giving blood, organ donation, nursing, or any corporal act of mercy that involves the body, such as feeding the hungry, caring for the sick, visiting the elderly, etc.

9. No. Generosity requires sacrifice—a willingness to renounce one's own will and suffer for another.

10. The world tells us that sacrifice is a bad thing, to be avoided at all cost. Scripture tells us that sacrifice is necessary to achieve eternal happiness, as well as to do good in the here and now. It also tells us that a willingness to sacrifice is the right response of a loving and grateful heart.

11. a–c. Take time to reflect and, if you are in a study group, prepare to share and discuss.

Lesson 3:
Prayer: The Fuel of Generosity

1.
Catechism, no. 2559: "'Prayer is the raising of one's mind and heart to God or the requesting of good things from God'" (St. John Damascene).
Catechism, no. 2565: "The life of prayer is the habit of being in the presence of the thrice-holy God and in communion with him."

2.
  a. The virtue of humility informs our hearts and wills of our complete and utter dependence upon God. When we recognize our dependence and need for God, we pray.
  b. God hears the prayers of the humble.
  c. Take time to reflect and, if you are in a study group, prepare to share your thoughts.

3.   James 5:13–14: When we have faith, we realize that God is concerned with us in both good times and bad. All circumstances are opportunities to pray. Furthermore, faith informs us that God is the one who is ultimately in control and prayer is our acknowledgement of this fact.

4.   David expresses profound humility and complete trust in the Lord. His response to humility and faith is prayer.

5.   We will receive what we are asking.

6.

Reference Verses	Prayer Form
Luke 1:62–64 Luke 2:25–35 Psalm 103:1–5	**Blessing & Adoration:** (See Catechism, nos. 2626–2628) These are prayers that acknowledge the wonder and magnificence of God.
1 John 3:21–22 1 John 1:8–10 James 1:5–8	**Petition:** (See Catechism, nos. 2629–2633.) These are our spontaneous requests of God, either for His blessings or forgiveness.
Numbers 14:13–20 James 5:16 Colossians 4:12 Romans 8:26	**Intercession:** (See Catechism, nos. 2634–2636.) These are the requests we make for the benefit of others.
1 Thessalonians 5:18 Romans 8:16 2 Corinthians 2:14 Psalm 118:1	**Thanksgiving:** (See Catechism, nos. 2637–2638.) These are our prayers for gratitude.
Ephesians 1:3 Revelation 5:11–14 Psalm 100 Psalm 98 Psalm 113	**Praise:** (See Catechism, nos. 2639–2643.) This is when we acknowledge and honor God for who He is.

7.

    a.   Take time to reflect and, if you are in a study group, prepare to share your experience.

    b.   Our real problem is that we do not accurately perceive our need for Christ or prayer. Ultimately it is a lack of humility and a lack of love. See Catechism, nos. 2728 and 2732. See also 1 Peter 5:5.

    c.   We must move our wills to do what we know is right. Virtue grows by exercising it, and our will to pray increases by praying.

8.

    a.   Martha's priorities were serving the meal and getting the house ready. Her priorities, however, cost her the opportunity to spend time with Jesus.

    b.   Mary's priority was listening to Jesus.

    c and d.   Take time to reflect and, if you are in a study group, prepare to share your experience and thoughts.

9. Take time to reflect and, if you are in a study group, prepare to share your story.

10.

    a.   Take time to reflect and, if you are in a study group, prepare to share your ideas.

    b.   It takes courage to give time when you are very busy, because you run the risk of neglecting something important. You have to trust that God will help you find the time later to deal with everything that is truly important.

    c.   Take time to reflect and to make any needed resolutions.

Lesson 4:
Family Life, Part I: "Till Death Do Us Part"—
Our Relationship with Our Spouse

1.
  a. We can recall the words of the *Baltimore Catechism*, "Why did God make me?" "God made me to know Him, to love Him and serve Him in this world and to be happy with Him forever in heaven." A fuller explanation is contained in the Catechism, nos. 356–361. (Please read this section—responses here are a feeble summary.) To be made in the image and likeness of God means that man can know and love God. It also means that he is called to share in the life of God. Sharing the life of God means that he is a person who can have both "self-knowledge," "self-possession," and "freely give himself and enter into communion with other persons." He is called to a covenant relationship with God.
  b. (1) "Be fruitful and multiply"—have children. (2) "Fill the earth and subdue it"—use your personal resources and the resources of earth to create and make beautiful things. (3) "Have dominion over . . . every living thing"—man is in charge of the creatures of the earth and a steward of them.

2. "It is not good that the man should be alone." God created us as social beings to live in communion with Him and one another.

3.
  a. A helper is an aid, someone who comes alongside another.
  b. The helper is made for both "man" in general and the man individually.

4. a–c. Take time to reflect and, if you are in a study group, prepare to share your thoughts and ideas.
5. A man and woman come of age and are to fulfill their adult

mission in the world. "It is not good for man to be alone"; so God provides a spouse. They "leave" their parents' home and "cleave" to the spouse. This is a mature move—from the security of the parents' home to a permanent bond with a "helpmate"—in the fulfillment of their mutual mission of fruitfulness and productivity in this world.

6. We are called to love. This love images the love of God. We are called to a fruitful love and the care for God's creation.

7.
   a. Mutual subjection is a dying to self and selfishness. To truly be another's helper you must think of your spouse's needs and often put his needs and desires before your own.
   b. It is a school of love because this dying to ourselves teaches us true love.
   c. It is hard to die to ourselves and put another first. We naturally seek to serve ourselves first.

8. Avoiding the temptation and providing accountability are the first and best means at your disposal. An honest, yet discreet and general, dialogue with your husband about these types of temptations can help to alert you to the level of issue it may be for your son(s) and husband. Strict control over the potential sources of pornography is a must. Simply do not allow it in your home, in any form, ever. Computers should be located in common family rooms, equipped with software that blocks such content, and updated regularly. You and your daughters can show self respect by dressing modestly. You can teach your daughter to honor her brothers in Christ by dressing and behaving in a way that does not tempt them to sin but rather honors the dignity of each.

9. a and b. Take time to reflect and, if you are in a study group, prepare to share your experience and ideas.

Lesson 5:
Family Life, Part II: The Gift of Children

1.

- a. Genesis 21:1–2 "The LORD did to Sarah as he had promised. And Sarah conceived."
- b. Genesis 30:1–2: "Am I in the place of God, who has withheld from you the fruit of the womb?"
- c. 1 Samuel 1:5 "because the LORD had closed her womb."
- d. Psalm 113:9 "He gives the barren woman a home, making her the joyous mother of children."

All of these verses clearly express that God is the creator of children.

2.

Matthew 19:13–15: (a) Jesus tenderly receives the children and shows that they are of great worth to Him. He lays His hands on them. (b) In this verse, Jesus teaches us that the child-like (those with faith and sincerity) will inherit heaven.

Mark 9:35–37: (a) We can just imagine Jesus holding and cuddling this young child. Children are so valued by Our Lord that He promises those who welcome children are welcoming Him. (b) Here, Jesus tells the apostles that in order to be first, they must be a servant of all. To illustrate the point, He brings forth a child and sets before them the example of how they are to serve—receive a child, serve a child. And in serving the child, we serve Christ. Jesus will repeat this message time and again. By accepting and serving the weak of the world, we serve Our Lord.

3.

- a. A blessing and reward.
- b. A home full of children is a sign of God's blessing.

4.

- a. A child is a gift. No one has the right to a child.

b. A child has the right to be conceived if God wills him to come forth as the fruit of conjugal love. A child also has "the right to be respected as a person from the moment of his conception." Children are not property or toys.

5. Notice that God punished him for *what* he did (spilled his semen) and not merely for *why* he did it (to dishonor his brother).

6. A child is the fulfillment of the love given to the spouses by God for one another. It is the fruit of that love. The marital act, as designed by God, is meant to both unite the spouses to one another and allow them to join with the Creator in creating a new life. These two ends may not be separated.

7. *Humanae Vitae* says that it is permissible to use natural family planning for grave reasons including physical, psychological, or "external" circumstances. The *Catechism of the Catholic Church* counsels that we may regulate births for just reasons but to be sure that these are not "motivated by selfishness" but, rather, we are encouraged to be generous and responsible.

8. Allow the women to share responses. The use of artificial birth control and surgical sterilization are serious sins and, if they have been used, it is important to repent and go to Confession. It is also important to remember that God is abundant in mercy and is always waiting to pick us up when we fall. All we must do is be willing to get up! Prayerful consideration of the motivations for not having a child must be considered (see question 7), and if it is determined that a birth must be spaced, natural family planning can be utilized.

9.

a–c. All of these passages prioritize the religious education of children. Parents are to pass on to their children the stories of God's faithfulness, provisions, and the importance of obeying Him.

d. Family prayer and devotions, taking the opportunity of "teachable moments" to explain the faith and encourage virtue in the context of real life—faith is not just for Sunday; it is meant to inform every aspect of our lives—home catechesis, involving them in parish life.

10. Teaching our children that God has a wonderful plan for their life is the first place to start. They should be aware that God may call them to religious life or married life and that they need to engage in a process of discernment. They should know that life is about more than what job they have, that it is ultimately about journeying to their heavenly home. What path does God want them to take?

11.
a. While parents are to instruct their children and discipline them, they are cautioned to not be overbearing or harsh.
b. Young children require patience, patience, and more patience. My young children always respond best when I am serene, lower my tone, and speak clearly and firmly. I do not have grown children yet and can only take my parents' example which I think has been a good one. They offer respectful guidance when I ask or when they think it is needed. However, they have never pushed or attempted to manipulate us. Now that we are adults, they treat us like adults.

12. Laying down our lives for others, springing from our faith, hope, and love for Jesus, is the heart of the Gospel message and a sure path to heaven. Living the Church's teaching on children gives us this opportunity.

Lesson 6:
Love Thy Neighbor

1.

  a. We tend to love ourselves more than anyone–with all our heart, soul, mind, and strength. So if we love our neighbor like we love ourselves, we are loving them with all our heart, soul, mind, and strength, which is also how we are called to love God. Furthermore, we will learn through Jesus' other sermons that we love God by loving our neighbor.

  b. The scribe in Mark's gospel understands that love is the heart of God and, therefore, love can bring him closer to God than the law. Many Christians still try to bargain with God by doing what is mediocre or even wrong and then trying to make up for it by big checks or time at Church, etc. Of course, it is important for us to give to the Church and make reparation for our sin. However, our motivation should be our love for God and not an attempt to manipulate Him.

2.

  a. We are fulfilling the moral law of God. We are being obedient to the will of God.

  b. Obedience is the first step to loving God; we cannot love if we are not first obedient.

3.

  a. We are to lay down our lives for "a friend."

  b. It means putting others' needs and wants before our own.

4.

  a. We can assume she is in the first trimester of her pregnancy with Jesus.

  b. Most likely, she traveled on foot or on the back of a donkey.

    c. She has come to help her aged cousin.

    d. Mary is going out of her way to help a family member in need when she may be tempted to allow others to serve her.

5.

    a. We can again assume that Mary is helping to serve at the wedding, and she noticed they were low on wine because she was observant of the needs of others.

    b. Mary was paying attention to the needs and desires of those around her. She did not want the wedding couple to embarrass themselves by running out of wine.

    c. Pay attention to the needs of those around us and go out of our way to meet those needs or help those needs to be met.

6.

    a. Jesus was exhausted.

    b. Jesus took the opportunity, despite His own exhaustion, to minister to the needs of the Samaritan woman. He put the needs of the woman of Samaria before His own.

    c. We are to serve even when we are tired or when we do not feel like it. We do it because it is right and because we love our neighbor out of our love for Jesus. Whatever we do to the least of our brothers we do for Him!

7. Take time to reflect and, if you are in a study group, prepare to share your ideas.

8. The parable teaches that we have all been forgiven much, and more than what any other human could possibly owe to us. If we do not forgive those around us, we are like the ungrateful servant who refuses to give even a little mercy after he has been given great mercy. The result is that he has to pay the full penalty or, rather, there is no forgiveness of the debt. We cannot receive God's forgiveness, if we will not forgive those who offend us.

9.

  a. Our pride and insecurities are two of the reasons why it is easy for us to judge our neighbor quickly. We want to feel good about ourselves or we think we are in a place to judge our neighbors. Usually when we fall into this sin we are puffed up with pride. We lack humility and charity.

  b. Jesus tells us that we need to look at our own sins!

  c. Take time to reflect and, if you are in a study group, prepare to share your experience and ideas.

10.

  a. Love is the essential thing. We show love to our neighbor in patience, kindness, and humility. We are warned against being rude, jealous, boastful, irritable, resentful, insisting on our own way.

  b. We are to be respectful of each person in Christ, those of high honor and those without, and recognize that each is indispensable. We are a family in Christ and must work together in love.

  c. Do not lie, reconcile with your neighbor, speak good things that lift up one another, do not be bitter, do not slander, be kind, tenderhearted, and forgiving.

  d. Do not say anything bad about another, do not quarrel, be gentle and courteous.

11.

  a. (1) Think good of others first. (2) If we cannot think well, make sure that we understand the person correctly. Maybe we are misunderstanding them. (3) If what they think is in fact wrong, we are to try to correct the misunderstanding in a loving way so that they may understand the truth. This is not done in the interest of self respect but for the sake of the other. (4) If a simple correction doesn't change their thinking, consider and try alternate methods to help them see their error.

b. Take time to reflect and, if you are in a study group, prepare to share your example.

12.

a. Jesus is telling Peter that he needs to keep his eyes fixed on Jesus and the path He has for him—not on John.

b. The lesson for us is to not worry about others' gifts or part in the body of Christ. We need to keep our eyes on Jesus and the mission we have.

Lesson 7:
Work and Money

1.
   a. God commands man to "subdue" the earth and to "till and keep" the Garden of Eden.
   b. They are given before the Fall.
   c. Work was part of God's plan from the beginning. It is not punishment for sin.

2.
   a. Work becomes "toil" and requires sweat.
   b. We complete the work of creation for our good and our neighbors'.

3.
   a. Work becomes a means of sanctification when we bear the hardships of it willingly and unite those struggles to Jesus' own struggles.
   b. Take time to reflect and, if you are in a study group, prepare to share your experience.
   c. These tasks allow us to put the interests of others ahead of our own. We can grow closer to Christ through these tasks by not putting them off, by not complaining about them, by performing them with a cheerful spirit, and by offering up the difficulties we face to Christ.

4.
   a. Everyone brings different and complementary gifts to the Body of Christ, making up for what is lacking in the other members.
   b and c. Take time to reflect and, if you are in a study group, prepare to share your experience and ideas.

5.

   a. (1) Be diligent. (2) Enjoy work and do it cheerfully. (3) Approach work with thoughtfulness and planning, as well as be teachable and seek out wise advice. (4) Work hard and know that in doing so, you're serving God.

   b. Jesus did not shirk manual labor or difficult work.

   c. Take time to reflect and, if you are in a study group, prepare to share your experience and ideas.

6.

   a. To be able to help others and to obtain the necessities of life. (Here, food is mentioned.)

   b. To guarantee our freedom and dignity, to meet our basic needs and the needs of those in our charge.

7. Good stewards do not borrow what they cannot pay back. They are generous and honest in all their transactions.

8.

   a. Love of money can lead us away from the faith, cause much suffering and strife, and prevent the Gospel from transforming us from within.

   b. Answers might include: fathers or mothers who sacrifice the good of their family for accumulating unnecessary wealth, people who profit off of others' sins (i.e. drug dealers, pornographers), people who spend beyond their means or borrow more than they can afford, or employers or executives who do not treat workers fairly in order to maximize their own profits.

   c. Answers might include broken homes, wounded children, pornography, the drug traffic, poverty, economic problems, or responsible people being forced to pay for the mistakes of the less responsible.

9.

a. We are tempted to trust in money.

b. We should trust in God.

c. God has promised He will not forsake us. He cares for even the littlest things in creation, and will care even more so for us, blessing those who trust in Him richly.

10.

a. Tithing was always meant to provide for the needs of the priests and to be an act of faith. Most likely, the people are not tithing because they do not have the faith that God will provide for their needs.

b. Of course God does not need their offerings. He requires it of them as a test of their faith and to build their faith. It is for *them* that they are required to tithe.

11.

a and b. The Pharisees are more concerned with externals. While the externals are important, they are merely outward signs of inward dispositions—our hearts. And God is more concerned with our heart. We are to give as a sign of our faith and love. The Pharisees were motivated by pride and self-righteousness.

12.

a. St. Paul echoes the teachings of Jesus and the importance of the disposition of our hearts. We are to give out of our love for God and the desire to see His Church and His people provided for.

b. God cannot be outdone in generosity. God will bless us abundantly for our offerings to His people.

13.

a. This is a personal reflection. If you are in a study group and are comfortable doing so, there may be opportunity to share your experience.

Lesson 8:
Sharing the Gospel

1. He commanded His disciples to baptize and preach to all nations.

2.
  a. He had compassion on them.
  b. He tells them to pray that God would send more workers.
  c. We are to pray for more workers and we *are* the workers. We should have compassion on the crowds that we see around us and share the love of God with them.

3. See answers on the next page.

3.

Passage	Who is Jesus helping?	What is their position in society?	Who is a modern parallel?	What is Jesus' message?
John 3:1–15	The Pharisee, Nicodemus.	Ruler and teacher of the Jews.	Religious leaders.	You must believe in Jesus and be born again.
John 4:6–26	Samaritan woman.	An outcast of her own people and a heretic in the eyes of Jews.	A cast out Muslim, Protestant, Jew etc.	I am the promised Savior.
John 7:37–44	The Jews.	Typical people.	Fellow Christians.	He is the promised Savior.
Matthew 9:9–13	Matthew, his fellow tax collectors, and other sinners.	The rejected and the despised.	Adulterers, prostitutes, other sinners.	I've come to save sinners.

4.
  a. Healing.
  b. Feeding.
  c. Working alongside His disciples.
  d. Preaching.
  e. Spending time with people.

5.
  a. The Gospel is to be preached to everyone, the righteous and the unrighteous, believers and non-believers, leaders and ordinary people.
  b. Jesus Christ is the Savior of the world.
  c. We communicate that through words and deeds, by preaching, serving others, and through forming relationships with people.
  d. He showed by meeting their corporal and spiritual needs that He loved them. He didn't shy away from speaking hard truths, but He was also gentle and loving when the situation called for it. He made people feel loved. Imitating him in those ways will make our own preaching more effective.

6.
  a. People can't believe in Christ if they have never heard of Him, and they can only hear about Him if those who know Him tell them.
  b. We preach out of necessity. The Gospel needs to be preached.
  c. God has entrusted us to preach the Gospel.
  d. To help people grow stronger in their faith.
  e. To help bring people to eternal life.

7.
  a. Do not follow the ways of the world; use our gifts for service to the Body of Christ; practice the virtues and be charitable.

   b. Bear with each other patiently and love one another as Christ loves us.

   c. Be a witness in the midst of the world.

   d. Trust in God and let others see our trust.

8–11. Take time to reflect and, if you are in a study group, prepare to share your thoughts, stories, and experiences.

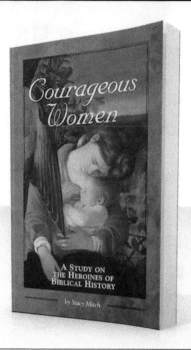

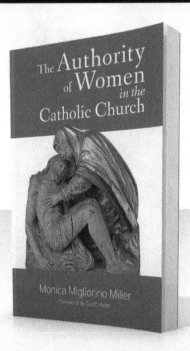

CPSIA information can be obtained
at www.ICGtesting.com
Printed in the USA
BVHW040145210821
614855BV00003B/82

9 781931 018579